MY FIRST JEWISH WORD BOOK

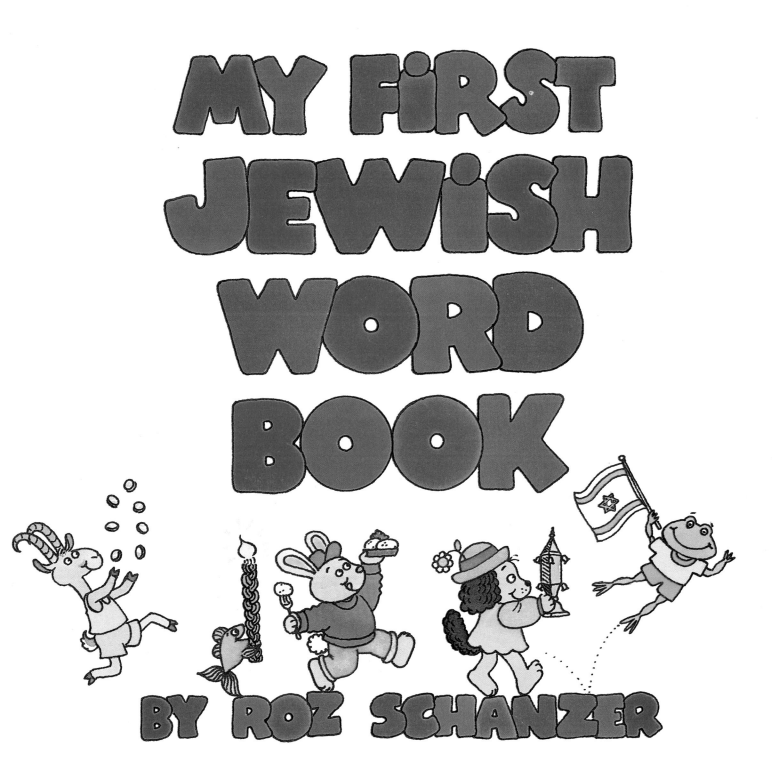

BY ROZ SCHANZER

KAR-BEN COPIES, INC.   ROCKVILLE, MD

For Beff
—R.S.

Library of Congress Cataloging-in-Publication Data

Schanzer, Rosalyn.
    My first Jewish work book/Rosalyn Schanzer.
       p.   cm.
    Summary: Text and captioned pictures depict the Jewish home, community, holidays, and symbols.
    ISBN 0-929371-36-4:
    1. Judaism—Customs and practices—Juvenile literature.   2. Fasts and feasts—Judaism—Juvenile
literature. [1. Judaism—Customs and practices.] I. Title.
    BM700.S29   1992
    296.4—dc20   92-12697
                                                             CIP
                                                             AC

Published by Kar-Ben Copies, Inc., Rockville, MD 1-800-4KARBEN
Printed in the United States of America.

etrog challah
grogger   tallit
                    seder
dreidel   Shabbat

MY FiRST
JEWiSH WORD BOOK

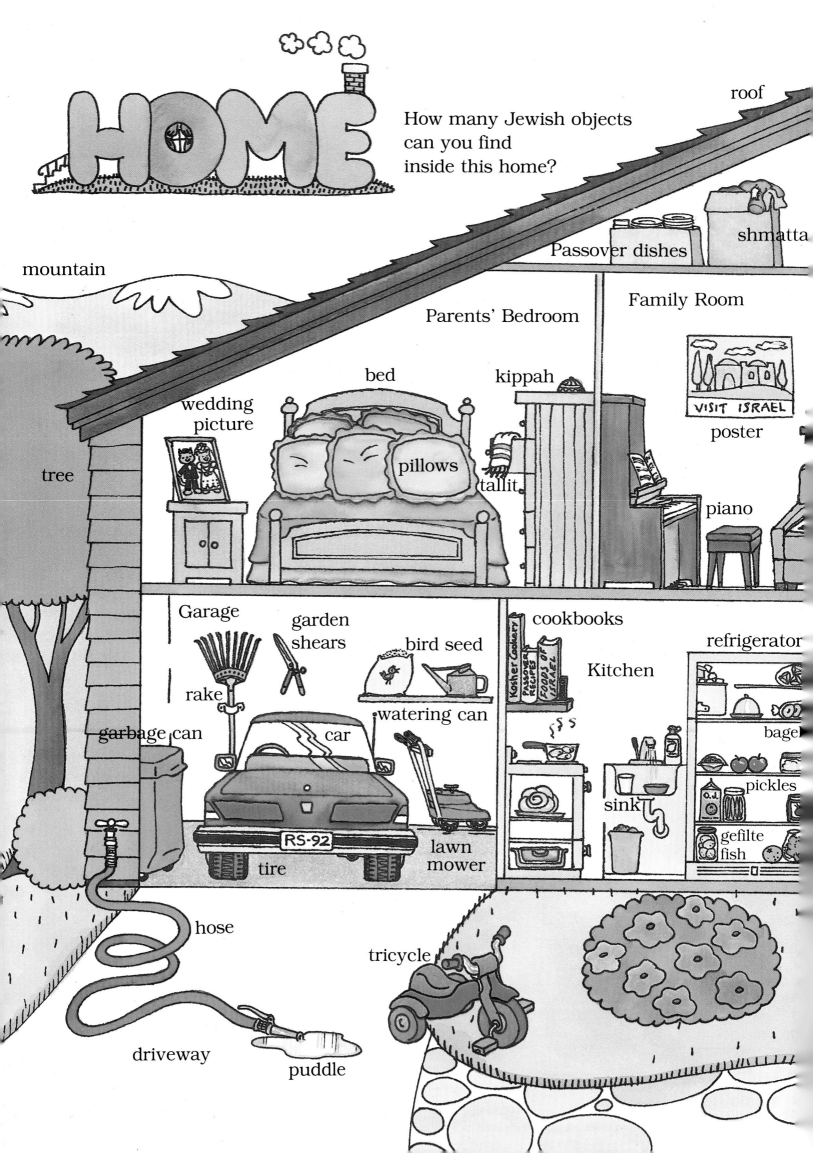

HOME

How many Jewish objects can you find inside this home?

roof

shmatta

Passover dishes

mountain

Family Room

Parents' Bedroom

bed

kippah

VISIT ISRAEL

poster

wedding picture

tree

pillows

tallit

piano

Garage

cookbooks

garden shears

refrigerator

bird seed

Kitchen

rake

watering can

bagel

garbage can

car

pickles

sink

RS-92

gefilte fish

lawn mower

tire

hose

tricycle

driveway

puddle

sun

cloud

attic

Purim costumes

chimney

calendar

Children's Bedroom

books

bunk bed

Israeli flag

ladder

tzedakah box

TV

toy

couch

dreidel

spice box

dishes

Living Room

photo

Dining Room

wine

candles

lamp

mezuzah

menorah

ddush cups

chair

bush

bee

tulips

path

SYNAGOGUE

We go to the synagogue to pray, to learn, and to celebrate.

Bat Mitzvah

stained glass windows

balcony

ner tamid

aron kodesh

SYNAGOGUE BETH-EL

Lobby

Sanctuary

Torah

kippot   prayer books

seats

bimah

tallitot

bush

Community

The Jewish community is a place
where people live, work, and play.

Shabbat

God made the world in six days and on the seventh day God rested. We call this day Shabbat.

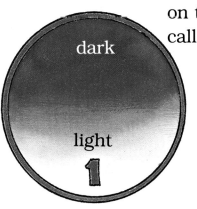

dark
light
1

sky
water
2

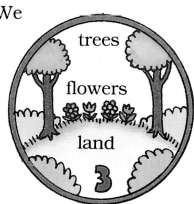

trees
flowers
land
3

sun   moon
stars
4

birds
fish
5

people
animals
6

margarine
sugar
flour
bowl
yeast
poppy seeds
apron
eggshells
measuring cup
challah
table

Making Challah

Lighting the Candles

flame

candlesticks

Blessing over the wine

Kiddush cup

Giving Tzedakah

tzedakah box

coin

Blessing over the bread

blessing

challah cover

challah

Havdallah

havdallah candle

wine cup

spice box

cotton tail

rug

stars

window

Rosh Hashanah
Yom Kippur

shanah tovah card

crayons

markers

mirror

price tag

dress

hat

purse

sales person

new clothes

dad

mom

sister

candles

guest

wine cup

kiss

pomegranate

round challah

honey

apples

brother

tablecloth

baby

At Home

Sound the shofar!
It's time to welcome
a sweet new year.

ner tamid

choir

aron kodesh

Torah

cantor

rabbi

shofar

bimah

kippah

tallit

hat

prayer books

congregation

In The Synagogue

SUKKOT

Preparing

Leafy branches and harvest fruits make our sukkah a perfect place to picnic.

paper chain

paper strips

popcorn

cap

needle

thread

cranberries

canvas

roof

ladder

wood

board

hammer

oy vey!

thumb

nails

Building the Sukkah

Decorating
the Sukkah

schach

carrot

gourd

grapes

apple

bee

pear

flowers

fruit

basket

corn stalks

star

lulav

etrog

bow

orange

pine cone

cup

table

chairs

ladybug

Celebrating
in the Sukkah

pumpkin

SIMCHAT TORAH

Israeli flag

flag

Let's celebrate! Dance, sing, and wave your flag. We've finished reading the Torah and are starting over again.

kippah

sharing

bow

polka dots

candy apple

rimonim

Parade

Torah

Torah Reading

Aliyah

Torah reader

tallit

gabbai

bimah

gabbai

Dancing

silver crown

mantle

yad

breastplate

wooden rollers

holding hands

HANUKKAH

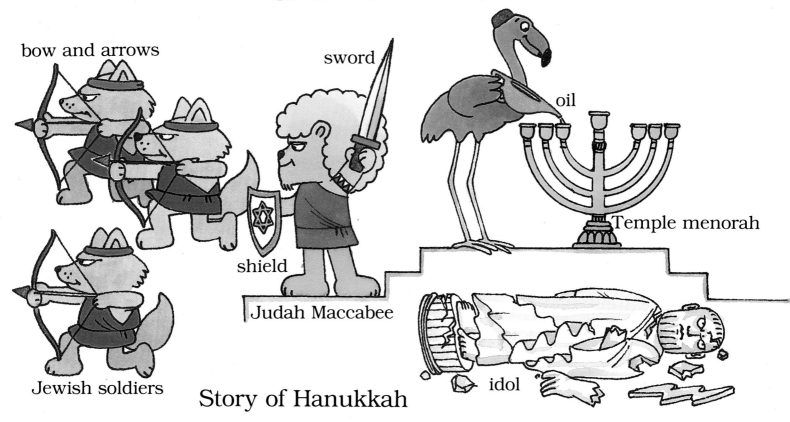

bow and arrows

sword

oil

Temple menorah

shield

Judah Maccabee

Jewish soldiers

idol

Story of Hanukkah

Making Potato Latkes

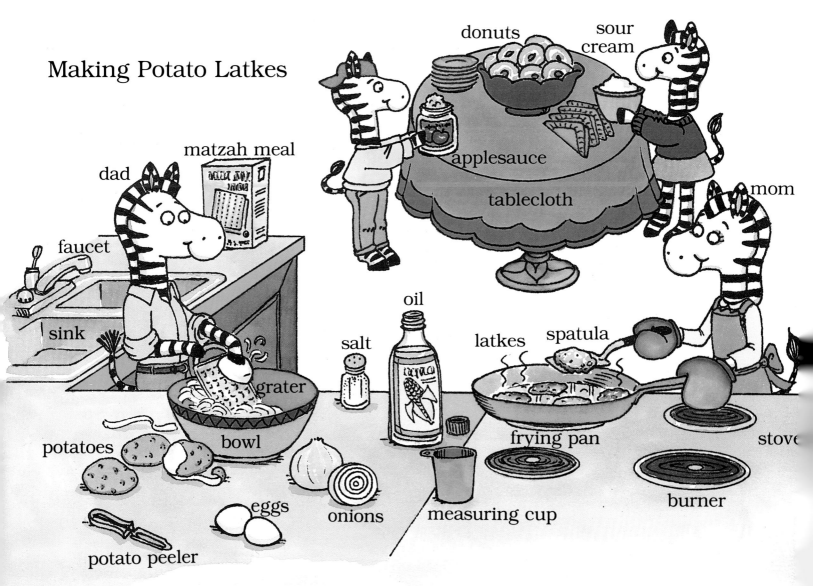

donuts

sour cream

dad

matzah meal

applesauce

tablecloth

mom

faucet

oil

sink

salt

latkes

spatula

grater

bowl

frying pan

stove

potatoes

eggs

onions

measuring cup

burner

potato peeler

Lighting the Hanukkah Candles

Each night we light one more candle to celebrate the victory of the Maccabees and the miracle of the oil.

shamash

hanukkiah

Opening Gifts

Thank you!

box

teddy bear

soccer ball

wrapping paper

bow

picture

ribbon

Playing Dreidel

dreidel

נ nun . . . . nothing
ג gimmel . . everything
ה hey . . . . . half
ש shin . . . . put in

peanuts

Hanukkah gelt

rain

forest

sun

Tu B'Shevat

Happy Birthday, trees!
Thank you for your
fruit and nuts,
shade and shelter.

butterfly

Planting

buds

watering can

spout

blossoms

sapling

shovel

grass

rake

gloves

hoe

seedlings

seeds

spade

Recycling

glass

compost bin

newspapers

Trees of Israel

leaves

lemon tree

coins

JNF box

cypress tree

pomegranate tree

branch

apple

trunk

olive tree

date palm

apple tree

Tasting Fruit

peanuts

peanut shell

peach

peach pit

strawberry

cherries

olives

dates

plum

grapefruit

blueberries

kiwi

coconut

fig

grapes

orange

We can eat all but the skin or shell.

We can eat all but the seed.

We can eat the whole fruit.

pot holder

oven

Purim

Baking Hamantaschen

grandpa

grandma

cap

poppy seed filling

salt

bowl

hamantaschen

rolling pin

cookie sheet

tiptoe

sugar

oil

flour

measuring cup

egg

spoon

three-cornered hat

sceptre

crown

grogger

King Ahashuerus

Haman

Purim Parade

hamantaschen costume

Delivering
Shalach Manot

chimney

cloud

roof

house

bird

tree

Reading
the Megillah

door

doorbell

mezuzah

kippah

grogger

cantor

yad

shalach manot
basket

megillah

mask

beard

rabbi

Vashti

Mordechai

Queen Esther

Purim is a time for merry-making and parades, as we
remember how brave Queen Esther saved the Jewish
people from wicked Haman.

Seder Plate

matzah cover

matzah

matzah ball soup

bone

charoset

egg

parsley

maror

Elijah's cup

wine

wine glasses

salt water

The special foods on the seder plate
help us tell the story of Passover.

Seder

rm chair

afikomen

illow

Asking the Four Questions

Haggadah

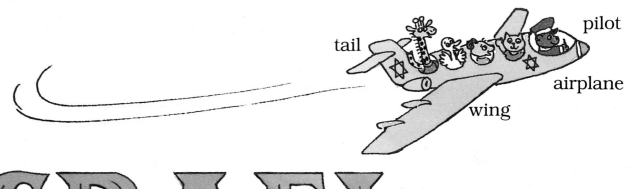

tail

pilot

airplane

wing

ISRAEL

Jerusalem

Dome of the Rock

The Kotel

Old City

praying

soldier

note

archway

pita bread

kefiyah

carpet

rice

oranges

baskets

brass pitcher

stool

The Shuk

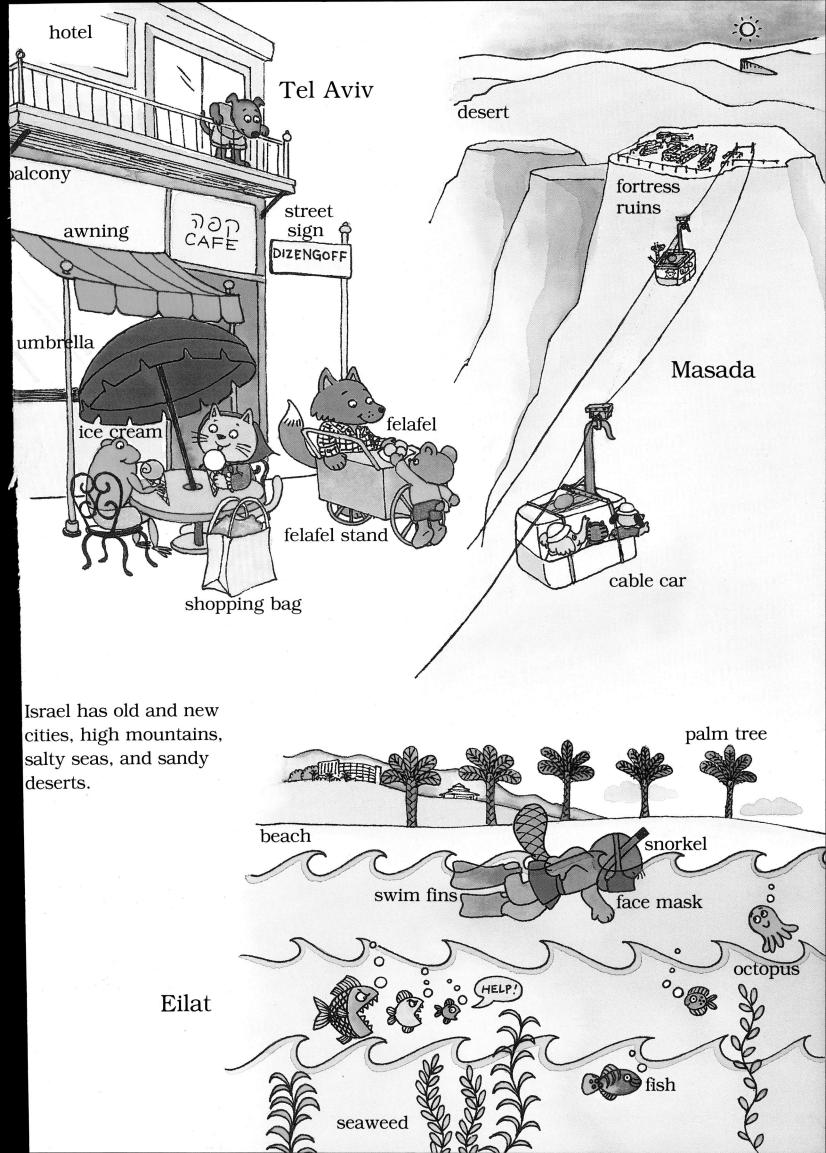

hotel

Tel Aviv

balcony

awning

קפה
CAFE

street sign

DIZENGOFF

umbrella

ice cream

felafel

felafel stand

shopping bag

desert

fortress ruins

Masada

cable car

Israel has old and new cities, high mountains, salty seas, and sandy deserts.

palm tree

beach

snorkel

swim fins

face mask

octopus

Eilat

HELP!

fish

seaweed

afikomen — matzah hidden to amuse children at the Passover seder

Ahashuerus — King of Persia who married Queen Esther (Purim story)

aliyah — the honor of reciting the Torah blessings

aron kodesh — holy ark where the Torah is kept in the synagogue

Bat Mitzvah — the coming of age for a Jewish girl, marked by a religious service and party

bimah — pulpit

cantor — person who chants prayers at a synagogue service

challah — braided egg bread eaten on Sabbath and holidays

chametz — bread and other foods which cannot be eaten during Passover

charoset — mixture of apples, nuts, and wine, eaten at the Passover seder to symbolize mortar used by Jewish slaves in Egypt

dreidel — four-sided top used in a Hanukkah game

Elijah's cup — goblet of wine set aside for the prophet Elijah at the Passover seder

etrog — citron; symbol of Sukkot

Four Questions — questions about Passover traditionally asked by the youngest at the seder

gabbai — synagogue official who supervises the reading of the Torah

grogger — noisemaker used on Purim to drown out the name of wicked Haman

haggadah — book containing the seder rituals and Passover story

Haman — Persian official who wished to kill the Jews on Purim

hamantaschen — three-cornered, filled cookies eaten on Purim (literally: Haman's pockets)

Hanukkah gelt — money given as a Hanukkah gift

Hanukkah menorah — 8-branched candelabra used on Hanukkah; also called hanukkiah

Havdallah — ceremony marking the end of the Sabbath

Havdallah candle — braided candle used at Havdallah

JNF box — collection box issued by Jewish National Fund, to raise money for trees in Israel

Judah Maccabee — hero of the Hanukkah story

kefiyah — Arab headdress

kiddush cup — wine cup

kippah — yarmulke, headcovering (plural: kippot)

kosher — fit to eat, according to Jewish law

lulav — palm branch bound with sprigs of myrtle and willow; Sukkot symbol

maror — bitter herb eaten at the Passover seder

matzah — unleavened bread eaten on Passover

megillah — scroll of Esther read on Purim

menorah — candelabra; the Temple menorah has 7 branches; the Hanukkah menorah has 8

mezuzah — parchment with Biblical passages which is attached to the doorposts of a Jewish home

Mordechai — cousin of Queen Esther (Purim story)

ner tamid — everlasting light that hangs over the holy ark in the synagogue

nun, gimmel, hey, shin — four Hebrew letters on the dreidel which stand for the Hebrew phrase "a great miracle happened there."

Passover dishes — special set of dishes used on Passover by traditional Jewish families

Pharaoh — king of Egypt

potato latkes — fried potato pancakes eaten on Hanukkah to recall the miracle of the oil

Queen Esther — Jewish queen of Persia; heroine of the Purim story

rabbi — teacher, congregational leader

rimonim — small silver Torah crowns (literally: pomegranates)

salt water — eaten at the Passover seder to recall the tears of Jewish slaves

schach — branches used to form the roof of the sukkah

seder plate — plate which holds the symbolic foods of the Passover seder

shalach manot — hamantaschen and sweets delivered to friends and family on Purim

shamash — helper candle used to light the Hanukkah candles

shanah tovah card — new year's card

shmattas — rags, old clothes (Yiddish)

shofar — ram's horn blown on the High Holidays

shuk — market

sukkah — harvest booth built on Sukkot

tallit — prayer shawl (plural: tallitot)

Torah — first five books of the Bible written on a parchment scroll

tzedakah — charitable gifts and good deeds (literally: justice)

tzedakah box — "bank" used to collect money for tzedakah

Vashti — first wife of King Ahashuerus (Purim story)

yad — pointer used to read the Torah